.75

A WAY OF LIFE

William Osler

A WAY OF LIFE: An Address delivered to Yale Students on the Evening of Sunday, April 20th, 1913, by WILLIAM OSLER, with a Foreword by Francis R. Packard. Published by Paul B. Hoeber Inc., Medical Book Department of Harper & Brothers, New York and London.

FOREWORD

In the spring of 1913 Osler came to the United States to deliver the Silliman Lectures at Yale University. Before coming he had promised to give a talk to the students and it is this "lay sermon" which is here reprinted. Cushing in his "Life of Osler" directs attention to the pressure under which it was written, although there is no evidence of any effort in its finish. He quotes from a note written by Osler on the original manuscript, "I wrote this on the steamer going to America, from notes that I had been jotting down for a month, but I only finished it on the Sunday of its delivery," and

Cushing adds that on the Saturday before he read the address Osler buried himself in the Graduates' Club at New Haven to complete his task, and that "the last seven of the nineteen pages of the manuscript from which he read, and from which the address was printed, are hand-written on paper of the Graduates' Club of New Haven."

The gist of Osler's sermon is a plea to do the day's work, to live in the day, and he tells how when a very young man he read Carlyle's familiar dictum: "Our main business is not to see what lies dimly at a distance, but to do what lies clearly at hand."

Cushing says that in a copy of the address in Osler's library the author had inscribed the following poem:

vi

"Listen to the Exhortation of the Dawn!
Look to this Day!
For it is Life, the very Life of Life.
In its brief Course lie all the
Varieties and Realities of your Existence:
The Bliss of Growth,
The Glory of Action,
The Splendour of Beauty;
For Yesterday is but a Dream
And Tomorrow is only a Vision;
But Today well lived makes
Every Yesterday a Dream of Happiness,
And every Tomorrow a Vision of Hope.
Look well therefore to this Day!
Such is the Salutation of the Dawn!"

Beneath the poem Osler had written "If

another reprint is called for put this on this page." We gladly comply with Sir William's suggestion that such an exquisite bit of verse should be recalled.

Francis R. Packard

A WAY OF LIFE

What each day needs that shalt thou ask,
Each day will set its proper task.

— *Goethe*

FELLOW STUDENTS:

Every man has a philosophy of life in thought, in word, or in deed, worked out in himself unconsciously. In possession of the very best, he may not know of its existence; with the very worst he may pride himself as a paragon. As it grows with the growth it cannot be taught to the young in formal lectures. What have bright eyes, red blood, quick breath and taut muscles to do with philosophy? Did not the great Stagirite say that young men were unfit students of it?—they will hear as though they heard not, and to no profit. Why then should I trouble you? Because I have a message that may be helpful. It is not philosophical, nor is it strictly moral or religious, one or other of which I was told my address should be, and yet in a way it is all three. It is the oldest and the freshest, the simplest and the most useful, so simple indeed is it that some of you may turn away disappointed as was Naaman the Syrian when told to go wash in Jordan and be clean. You know those composite tools to be bought for 50 cents, with one handle to fit a score or more of instruments. The workmanship is usually bad, so bad, as a rule, that you will not find an example in any

2

good carpenter's shop; but the boy has one, the chauffeur slips one into his box, and the sailor into his kit, and there is one in the odds-and-ends drawer of the pantry of every well-regulated family. It is simply a handy thing about the house, to help over the many little difficulties of the day. Of this sort of philosophy I wish to make you a present—a handle to fit your life tools. Whether the workmanship is Sheffield or shoddy, this helve will fit anything from a hatchet to a corkscrew.

My message is but a word, *a Way*, an easy expression of the experience of a plain man whose life has never been worried by any philosophy higher than that of the shepherd in *As You Like It*. I wish to point out a path in which the wayfaring man, though a fool,

3

cannot err; not a system to be worked out painfully only to be discarded, not a formal scheme, simply a habit as easy—or as hard!—to adopt as any other habit, good or bad.

A FEW years ago a Xmas card went the rounds, with the legend, "Life is just one 'derned' thing after another," which, in more refined language, is the same as saying, "Life is a habit," a succession of actions that become more or less automatic. This great truth, which lies at the basis of all actions, muscular or psychic, is the keystone to the teaching of Aristotle, to whom the formation of habits was the basis of moral excellence.

"In a word, habits of any kind are the result of actions of the same kind; and so what we have to do, is to give a certain character to these particular actions" (*Ethics*). Lift a seven months old baby to his feet—see him tumble on his nose. Do the same at twelve months— he walks. At two years he runs. The muscles and the nervous system have acquired the habit. One trial after another, one failure after another, has given him power. Put your finger in a baby's mouth, and he sucks away in bliss⁄ ful anticipation of a response to a mammalian habit millions of years old. And we can de⁄ liberately train parts of our body to perform complicated actions with unerring accuracy. Watch that musician playing a difficult piece. Batteries, commutators, multipliers, switches, wires innumerable control those nimble fingers, the machinery of which may be set in motion as automatically as in a pianola, the player all the time chatting as if he had nothing to do in controlling the apparatus — habit again, the gradual acquisition of power by long practice and at the expense of many mistakes. The same great law reaches through mental and moral states. "Character," which partakes of both, in Plutarch's words, is "longstanding habit."

Now the way of life that I preach is a habit to be acquired gradually by long and steady repetition. It is the practice of living for the day only, and for the day's work, *Life in daytight compartments.* "Ah," I hear you say, "that is an easy matter, simple as Elisha's advice!"

7

Not as I shall urge it, in words which fail to express the depth of my feelings as to its value. I started life in the best of all environments— in a parsonage, one of nine children. A man who has filled Chairs in four universities, has written a successful book, and has been asked to lecture at Yale, is supposed popularly to have brains of special quality. A few of my intimate friends really know the truth about me, as I know it! Mine, in good faith I say it, are of the most mediocre character. But what about those professorships, etc.? Just habit, a way of life, an outcome of the day's work, the vital importance of which I wish to impress upon you with all the force at my command.

Dr. Johnson remarked upon the trifling

circumstances by which men's lives are influenced, "not by an ascendant planet, a predominating humour, but by the first book which they read, some early conversation which they have heard, or some accident which excited ardour and enthusiasm." This was my case in two particulars. I was diverted to the Trinity College School, then at Weston, Ontario, by a paragraph in the circular stating that the senior boys would go into the drawing-room in the evenings, and learn to sing and dance—vocal and pedal accomplishments for which I was never designed; but like Saul seeking his asses, I found something more valuable, a man of the White of Selborne type, who knew nature, and who knew how to get boys interested in it. The other happened in the

9

summer of 1871, when I was attending the Montreal General Hospital. Much worried as to the future, partly about the final examination, partly as to what I should do afterwards, I picked up a volume of Carlyle, and on the page I opened there was the familiar sentence — *"Our main business is not to see what lies dimly at a distance, but to do what lies clearly at hand."* A commonplace sentiment enough, but it hit and stuck and helped, and was the starting point of a habit that has enabled me to utilize to the full the single talent entrusted to me.

II

THE workers in Christ's vineyard were hired by the day; only for this day are we to ask for our daily bread, and we are expressly bidden to take no thought for the morrow. To the modern world these commands have an Oriental savour, counsels of perfection akin to certain of the Beatitudes, stimuli to aspiration, not to action. I am prepared on the contrary to urge the literal acceptance of the advice, not in the mood of

11

St. James—"Go to now, ye that say, To-day or to-morrow we will go into such a city, and continue there a year, and buy and sell and get gain; whereas ye know not what shall be on the morrow"; not in the Epicurean spirit of Omar with his "jug of wine and thou," but in the modernist spirit, as a way of life, a habit, a strong enchantment at once against the mysticism of the East and the pessimism that too easily besets us. Change that hard saying "sufficient unto the day is the evil thereof," into "the goodness thereof," since the chief worries of life arise from the foolish habit of looking before and after. As a patient with double vision from some transient un-equal action of the muscles of the eye finds magical relief from well-adjusted glasses, so, returning to the clear binocular vision of to-day, the over-anxious student finds peace when he looks neither backward to the past nor forward to the future.

I stood on the bridge of one of the great liners, ploughing the ocean at 25 knots. "She is alive," said my companion, "in every plate; a huge monster with brain and nerves, an immense stomach, a wonderful heart and lungs, and a splendid system of locomotion." Just at that moment a signal sounded, and all over the ship the water-tight compartments were closed. "Our chief factor of safety," said the captain. "In spite of the *Titanic*," I said. "Yes," he replied, "in spite of the *Titanic*." Now each one of you is a much more marvellous organization than the great liner, and bound on a longer voyage. What I urge is that you so learn to control the machinery as to live with "day-tight compartments" as the most certain way to ensure safety on the voyage. Get on the bridge and see that at least the great bulkheads are in working order. Touch a button and hear, at every level of your life, the iron doors shutting out the Past—the dead yesterdays. Touch another and shut off, with a metal curtain, the Future—the unborn to-morrows. Then you are safe—safe for to-day! Read the old story in the *Chambered Nautilus*, so beautifully sung by Oliver Wendell Holmes, only change one line to "Day after day behold the silent toil." Shut off the past. "Let the dead past bury its dead." So easy to say, so hard to realize! The truth is, the past haunts us like a shadow. To disregard it is not easy. Those blue eyes of your grandmother, that weak chin of your grandfather, have mental and moral counterparts in your make-up. Generations of ancestors, brooding over "Providence, foreknowledge, will and fate, Fixed fate, free will, foreknowledge absolute," may have bred a New England conscience, morbidly sensitive, to heal which some of you had rather sing the 51st Psalm than follow Christ into the slums. Shut out the yesterdays, which have lighted fools the way to dusty death, and have no concern for you personally, that is, consciously. They are there all right, working daily in us, but so are our livers and our stomachs. And the past, in its unconscious action on our lives, should bother

15

us as little as they do. The petty annoy-
ances, the real and fancied slights, the trivial
mistakes, the disappointments, the sins, the
sorrows, even the joys—bury them deep in the
oblivion of each night. Ah! but it is just then
that to so many of us the ghosts of the past,

> Night-riding Incubi
> Troubling the fantasy,

come in troops, and pry open the eyelids,
each presenting a sin, a sorrow, a regret. Bad
enough in the old and seasoned, in the young
these demons of past sins may be a terrible
affliction, and in bitterness of heart many a one
cries with Eugene Aram, "Oh God! Could
I so close my mind, and clasp it with a clasp."
As a vaccine against all morbid poisons left

in the system by the infections of yesterday, I offer "a way of life." "Undress," as George Herbert says, "your soul at night," not by self-examination, but by shedding, as you do your garments, the daily sins whether of omission or of commission, and you will wake a free man, with a new life. To look back, except on rare occasions for stock-taking, is to risk the fate of Lot's wife. Many a man is handicapped in his course by a cursed combination of retro- and intro-spection, the mistakes of yesterday paralysing the efforts of to-day, the worries of the past hugged to his destruction, and the worm Regret allowed to canker the very heart of his life. To die daily, after the manner of St. Paul, ensures the resurrection of a new man, who makes each day the epitome of life.

17

III

THE load of to-morrow added to that of yesterday, carried to-day, makes the strongest falter. Shut off the future as tightly as the past. No dreams, no visions, no delicious fantasies, no castles in the air, with which, as the old song so truly says, "hearts are broken, heads are turned." To youth, we are told, belongs the future, but the wretched to-morrow that so plagues some of us has no certainty, except through to-day. Who can

18

tell what a day may bring forth? Though its uncertainty is a proverb, a man may carry its secret in the hollow of his hand. Make a pilgrimage to Hades with Ulysses, draw the magic circle, perform the rites, and then ask Tiresias the question. I have had the answer from his own lips. The future is to-day—there is no to-morrow! The day of a man's salvation is *now*—the life of the present, of to-day, lived earnestly, intently, without a forward-looking thought, is the only insurance for the future. Let the limit of your horizon be a twenty-four hour circle. On the title page of one of the great books of science, the *Discours de la Methode* of Descartes (1637), is a vignette showing a man digging in a garden with his face towards the earth, on which rays of light are streaming

19

from the heavens; above him is the legend *"Fac et Spera"* 'Tis a good attitude and a good motto. Look heavenward, if you wish, but never to the horizon—that way danger lies. Truth is not there, happiness is not there, certainty is not there, but the falsehoods, the frauds, the quackeries, the *ignes fatui* which have deceived each generation—all beckon from the horizon, and lure the men not content to look for the truth and happiness that tumble out at their feet. Once while at College climb a mountain top, and get a general outlook of the land, and make it the occasion perhaps of that careful examination of yourself, that inquisition which Descartes urges every man to hold once in a lifetime—not oftener.

Waste of energy, mental distress, nervous

worries dog the steps of a man who is anxious about the future. Shut close, then, the great fore and aft bulkheads, and prepare to cultivate the habit of a life of Day-Tight Compartments. Do not be discouraged—like every other habit, the acquisition takes time, and the way is one you must find for yourselves. I can only give general directions and encouragement, in the hope that while the green years are on your heads, you may have the courage to persist.

IV

NOW, for the day itself! What first? Be your own daysman! and sigh not with Job for any mysterious intermediary, but prepare to lay your own firm hand upon the helm. Get into touch with the finite, and grasp in full enjoyment that sense of capacity in a machine working smoothly. Join the whole creation of animate things in a deep heartfelt joy that you are alive, that you see the sun, that you are in this glorious earth

22

which nature has made so beautiful, and which is yours to conquer and to enjoy. Realize, in the words of Browning, that "There's a world of capability for joy spread round about us, meant for us, inviting us." What are the morning sensations?—for they control the day. Some of us are congenitally unhappy during the early hours; but the young man who feels on awakening that life is a burden or a bore has been neglecting his machine, driving it too hard, stoking the engines too much, or not cleaning out the ashes and clinkers. Or he has been too much with the Lady Nicotine, or fooling with Bacchus, or, worst of all, with the younger Aphrodite—all "messengers of strong prevailment in unhardened youth." To have a sweet outlook on life you must have a

23

clean body. As I look on the clear-cut, alert, earnest features, and the lithe, active forms of our college men, I sometimes wonder whether or not Socrates and Plato would find the race improved. I am sure they would love to look on such a gathering as this. Make their ideal yours—the fair mind in the fair body. The one cannot be sweet and clean without the other, and you must realize, with Rabbi Ben Ezra, the great truth that flesh and soul are mutually helpful. This morning outlook—which really makes the day—is largely a question of a clean machine—of physical morality in the wide sense of the term. *"C'est l'estomac qui fait les heureux,"* as Voltaire says; no dyspeptic can have a sane outlook on life; and a man whose bodily functions are impaired has a lowered

24

moral resistance. To keep the body fit is a help in keeping the mind pure, and the sensations of the first few hours of the day are the best test of its normal state. The clean tongue, the clear head, and the bright eye are birthrights of each day. Just as the late Professor Marsh would diagnose an unknown animal from a single bone, so can the day be predicted from the first waking hour. The start is everything, as you well know, and to make a good start you must feel fit. In the young, sensations of morning slackness come most often from lack of control of the two primal instincts — biologic habits — the one concerned with the preservation of the individual, the other with the continuance of the species. Yale students should by this time be models of dietetic propriety,

25

but youth does not always reck the rede of the teacher; and I dare say that here, as elsewhere, careless habits of eating are responsible for much mental disability. My own rule of life has been to cut out unsparingly any article of diet that had the bad taste to disagree with me, or to indicate in any way that it had abused the temporary hospitality of the lodging which I had provided. To drink, nowadays, but few students become addicted, but in every large body of men a few are to be found whose incapacity for the day results from the morning clogging of nocturnally flushed tissues. As moderation is very hard to reach, and as it has been abundantly shown that the best of mental and physical work may be done without alcohol in any form, the safest rule for the young man

26

is that which I am sure most of you follow—
abstinence. A bitter enemy to the bright eye
and the clear brain of the early morning is tobacco when smoked to excess, as it is now by
a large majority of students. Watch it, test it,
and if need be, control it. That befogged, woolly
sensation reaching from the forehead to the oc-
ciput, that haziness of memory, that cold fish-
like eye, that furred tongue and last week's
taste in the mouth—too many of you know
them—I know them—they often come from
too much tobacco. The other primal instinct
is the heavy burden of the flesh which Nature
puts on all of us to ensure a continuation of
the species. To drive Plato's team taxes the
energies of the best of us. One of the horses
is a raging, untamed devil, who can only be

27

brought into subjection by hard fighting and severe training. This much you all know as men; once the bit is between his teeth the black steed Passion will take the white horse Reason with you and the chariot rattling over the rocks to perdition.

With a fresh, sweet body you can start aright without those feelings of inertia that so often, as Goethe says, make the morning's lazy leisure usher in a useless day. Control of the mind as a working machine, the adaptation in it of habit, so that its action becomes almost as automatic as walking, is the end of education—and yet how rarely reached! It can be accomplished with deliberation and repose, never with hurry and worry. Realize how much time there is, how long the day is. Realize that

28

you have sixteen waking hours, three or four of which at least should be devoted to making a silent conquest of your mental machinery. Concentration, by which is grown gradually the power to wrestle successfully with any subject, is the secret of successful study. No mind however dull can escape the brightness that comes from steady application. There is an old saying, "Youth enjoyeth not, for haste"; but worse than this, the failure to cultivate the power of peaceful concentration is the greatest single cause of mental breakdown. Plato pities the young man who started at such a pace that he never reached the goal. One of the saddest of life's tragedies is the wreckage of the career of the young collegian by hurry, hustle, bustle and tension—the human machine driven day and night, as no sensible fellow would use his motor. Listen to the words of a master in Israel, William James: "Neither the nature nor the amount of our work is accountable for the frequency and severity of our breakdowns, but their cause lies rather in those absurd feelings of hurry and having no time, in that breathlessness and tension; that anxiety of feature and that solicitude of results, that lack of inner harmony and ease, in short, by which the work with us is apt to be accompanied, and from which a European who would do the same work would, nine out of ten times, be free." *Es bildet ein Talent sich in der Stille*, but it need not be for all day. A few hours out of the sixteen will suffice, only let them be hours of daily dedication—in routine, in order and in system, and day by day

30

you will gain in power over the mental mechanism, just as the child does over the spinal marrow in walking, or the musician over the nerve centres. Aristotle somewhere says that the student who wins out in the fight must be slow in his movements, with voice deep, and slow speech, and he will not be worried over trifles which make people speak in shrill tones and use rapid movements. Shut close in hour-tight compartments, with the mind directed intensely upon the subject in hand, you will acquire the capacity to do more and more, you will get into training; and once the mental habit is established you are safe for life.

Concentration is an art of slow acquisition, but little by little the mind is accustomed to habits of slow eating and careful digestion, by

31

which alone you escape the "mental dyspepsy" so graphically described by Lowell in the *Fable for Critics*. Do not worry your brains about that bugbear Efficiency, which, sought consciously and with effort, is just one of those elusive qualities very apt to be missed. The man's college output is never to be gauged at sight; all the world's coarse thumb and finger may fail to plumb his most effective work, the casting of the mental machinery of self-education, the true preparation for a field larger than the college campus. Four or five hours daily—it is not much to ask; but one day must tell another, one week certify another, one month bear witness to another of the same story, and you will acquire a habit by which the one-talent man will earn a high interest, and by which the ten-talent man may at least save his capital.

Steady work of this sort gives a man a sane outlook on the world. No corrective so valuable to the weariness, the fever and the fret that are so apt to wring the heart of the young. This is the talisman, as George Herbert says,

> The famous stone
> That turneth all to gold,

and with which, to the eternally recurring question, What is Life? you answer, I do not think—I act it; the only philosophy that brings you in contact with its real values and enables you to grasp its hidden meaning. Over the Slough of Despond, past Doubting Castle and Giant Despair, with this talisman you may reach the Delectable Mountains, and those

Shepherds of the Mind—Knowledge, Experience, Watchful and Sincere. Some of you may think this to be a miserable Epicurean doctrine—no better than that so sweetly sung by Horace:—

> Happy the man—and Happy he alone,
> He who can call to-day his own,
> He who secure within can say,
> To-morrow, do thy worst—for I have
> lived to-day.

I do not care what you think, I am simply giving you a philosophy of life that I have found helpful in my work, useful in my play. Walt Whitman, whose physician I was for some years, never spoke to me much of his poems, though occasionally he would make a quotation;

but I remember late one summer afternoon as we sat in the window of his little house in Camden there passed a group of workmen whom he greeted in his usual friendly way. And then he said: "Ah, the glory of the day's work, whether with hand or brain! I have tried

To exalt the present and the real,
To teach the average man the glory of his
daily work or trade."

In this way of life each one of you may learn to drive the straight furrow and so come to the true measure of a man.

V

WITH body and mind in training, what remains?

Do you remember that most touching of all incidents in Christ's ministry, when the anxious ruler Nicodemus came by night, worried lest the things that pertained to his everlasting peace were not a part of his busy and successful life? Christ's message to him is His message to the world—never more needed than at present: "Ye must be born of the

36

spirit." You wish to be with the leaders—as Yale men it is your birthright—know the great souls that make up the moral radium of the world. You must be born of their spirit, initiated into their fraternity, whether of the spiritually-minded followers of the Nazarene or of that larger company, elect from every nation, seen by St. John.

Begin the day with Christ and His prayer —you need no other. Creedless, with it you have religion; creed-stuffed, it will leaven any theological dough in which you stick. As the soul is dyed by the thoughts, let no day pass without contact with the best literature of the world. Learn to know your Bible, though not perhaps as your fathers did. In forming character and in shaping conduct, its touch has still its ancient power. Of the kindred of Ram and sons of Elihu, you should know its beauties and its strength. Fifteen or twenty minutes day by day will give you fellowship with the great minds of the race, and little by little as the years pass you extend your friendship with the immortal dead. They will give you faith in your own day. Listen while they speak to you of the fathers. But each age has its own spirit and ideas, just as it has its own manners and pleasures. You are right to believe that yours is the best University at its best period. Why should you look back to be shocked at the frowsiness and dullness of the students of the seventies or even of the nineties? And cast no thought forward, lest you reach a period where you and yours will

38

present to your successors the same dowdiness of clothes and times. But while change is the law, certain great ideas flow fresh through the ages, and control us effectually as in the days of Pericles. Mankind, it has been said, is always advancing, man is always the same. The love, hope, fear and faith that make humanity, and the elemental passions of the human heart, remain unchanged, and the secret of inspiration in any literature is the capacity to touch the cord that vibrates in a sympathy that knows nor time nor place.

The quiet life in day-tight compartments will help you to bear your own and others' burdens with a light heart. Pay no heed to the Batrachians who sit croaking idly by the stream. Life is a straight, plain business, and the way is clear, blazed for you by generations of strong men, into whose labours you enter and whose ideals must be your inspiration. In my mind's eye I can see you twenty years hence—resolute-eyed, broad-headed, smooth-faced men who are in the world to make a success of life; but to whichever of the two great types you belong, whether controlled by emotion or by reason, you will need the leaven of their spirit, the only leaven potent enough to avert that only too common Nemesis to which the Psalmist refers: "He gave them their heart's desire, but sent leanness withal into their souls."

I quoted Dr. Johnson's remark about the trivial things that influence. Perhaps this slight word of mine may help some of you so to number your days that you may apply your hearts unto wisdom.

Hand-set in Goudy Mediæval
type by Arthur and Edna Rushmore at The
Golden Hind Press in Madison, New Jersey,
for Paul B. Hoeber, Inc. in New York City.